Author: Kate Melton

Disclaimer and Terms of Use:
Effort has been made to ensure that the information in this book is accurate and complete, however, the author and the publisher do not warrant the accuracy of the information, text and graphics contained within the book due to the rapidly changing nature of science, research, known and unknown facts and internet. The Author and the publisher do not hold any responsibility for errors, omissions or contrary interpretation of the subject matter herein. This book is presented solely for motivational and informational purposes only.

Cutie Sue

and
the Christmas Miracle

Kate Melton

illustrated by
Ira Baykovska

Christmas was coming,
the streets looked so bright,
So Sue grabbed a pen
and she started to write.

Dear Santa,

she wrote, making sure to be neat,
Everyone knows that you're caring and sweet.

This is the list of the things I would like:
A couple of books and a shiny new bike.

A dollhouse, a tablet, a new sequined top,
Just like the one that I saw in the shop.

A train set, a ball, and a new talking doll,
But there is one thing I would like above all...

A miracle, Santa, that money can't buy,
I'd like to see snow flurry down from the sky.

So, we can toboggan and build snowmen too!
I hope you can do it.

Your dear Cutie Sue

She posted her letter and looked at the sky,
"I hope my plan works," whispered Sue with a sigh.

"But Christmas," she said, "feels like ages away!"
So, she tried to keep busy whilst counting the days.

She helped to wrap presents and clean up the floor,
She made a new wreath to put up on the door.

She played with her brother; the two got along,
She helped Mom bake cookies
and sang Christmas songs.

She adorned every room
and she signed every card,
And, soon, all that waiting
did not feel too hard!

The day before Christmas had finally come,
They all celebrated, but Cutie was glum.

She just couldn't help it
but felt rather blue,
"My wish," she said, worried,
"might not become true!"

The following day Cutie shouted,
"Wow-wee!"
There were all sorts of presents
tucked under the tree.

She got all the gifts
that she said she would like,
A couple of books and a shiny new bike.

A dollhouse, a tablet, a new sequined top,
Just like the one she had seen in the shop.

A train set, a ball, and a new talking doll,
"But where is the thing I would like most of all?"

She looked out the window and searched all around,
"No snow," whispered Cutie, inspecting the ground.

The girl was distraught, "This is hopeless!" she cried,
"I won't get my miracle," Cutie Sue sighed.

"Darling," said Mom, "you shouldn't feel sad,
YOU can make miracles happen instead.

"There's so much to do all around us, you know?
Some people are lonely and feel rather low.

"They long for a friend who can pay them a call,
This is what Christmas' about after all!"

"Oh, I didn't know!" said Cutie wide-eyed,
So, she put on her coat and she marched right outside.

"I'll visit my neighbor who's lonely this year,
He's ever so nice and he needs some good cheer."

She knocked on his door and she gave him a treat,
"Thanks!" he said softly, "That's ever so sweet!"

She found a stray dog sitting all on his own,
She gave him a pat and a big, juicy bone.

The dog munched it up; he no longer looked frail,
He thanked Cutie Sue with a wag of his tail.

She saw her friend Ben,
they'd had a big fight,
"It's time," whispered Sue,
"Ben and I make things right."

So, she gave him a gift, "It's my favorite book,"
"Thank you," said Ben with a touched, thankful look.

"It's snowing!" she bellowed,
"My wish has come true!"
Mom gave a smile,
"Well done, Cutie Sue!"

Santa peered down from his magical sleigh,
And saw just how hard Cutie Sue worked all day.

"My dear little helper," he said feeling proud,
Then Zoom! off he flew, through the thick,
snowy clouds.

www.ingramcontent.com/pod-product-compliance
Lightning Source LLC
Chambersburg PA
CBHW042003100426
42813CB00020B/2972